Dear Cookie &

Thanks for your v.
in my book! Look fo
to March 2007 and to
you both at Lehigh Rea

Love,
Shirley

Riding on God's Coattails

Riding on God's Coattails

Shirley A. Tindall

VANTAGE PRESS
New York

Front cover photo: The author, her youngest daughter, and grandson—three generations—water-skiing. The author's middle daughter piloted the boat pulling the skiers. Photo by Dave Carlson, *Muskegon Chronicle,* used by permission.

Excerpts taken from Elaine Youngs' letter are used by permission.

FIRST EDITION

All rights reserved, including the right of reproduction in whole or in part in any form.

Copyright © 2006 by Shirley A. Tindall

Published by Vantage Press, Inc.
419 Park Ave. South, New York, NY 10016

Manufactured in the United States of America
ISBN: 0-533-15252-6

Library of Congress Catalog Card No.: 2005904675

0 9 8 7 6 5 4 3 2 1

Contents

Acknowledgments	vii
Prologue	1
I. Grandparents on Mother's Side	3
II. Grandparents on Father's Side	4
III. Father	7
IV. Mother	10
V. First Born	18
VI. Second Born	24
VII. Third Born	40
VIII. Fourth Born and Author of This Book	43
IX. Fifth Born	70
X. Sixth Born	73
XI. Leaving a Heritage and Staying on God's Coattails!	76
Questionnaire	81

Acknowledgments

Books I took out of the Hackley Public Library in Muskegon, Michigan were *Dialogue,* Lewis Tures; *Guide to Fiction Writing,* Phyllis A. Whitney; and *Voice Power,* Evelyn Burge; each helped me to use more descriptive words.

I sent out questionnaires to my three surviving siblings for any important information about my family before I was born. I received a letter from my brother Bob's widow helping clear up some questions I had about their relationship with my oldest sister and her husband.

I thank Elaine Youngs for the letter she sent me when Dave, my first husband, passed away. Also, I am sharing the "Love Story" written by my mother-in-law, step-mother of Dave.

I thank my children for being so encouraging and my son and daughter-in-law for putting the book on a computer disk; my daughter-in-law for generously offering to type my story for me; my daughter, Kathy, for faxing many a query letter to publishers and the many friends; and my book club, who encouraged me to write my story.

Riding on God's Coattails

Prologue

This book is about my family and how my life was influenced by them.

I start with a little information about my great-grandfather, on my father's side, and continue with grandparents on both my mother's and father's sides. I detail my life because of my walk as a Christian. I always tried to keep communications open, sharing knowledge so we (siblings) could help one another as we aged. I am a middle child and a peacemaker. Sharing our heritage is also important. Because of my second marriage, this became even more important. The family heirlooms should be passed down from generation to generation.

Genealogy is not the most important aspect, but how the influences of grandparents, parents, and siblings shape our lives. We learn by others' actions, whether they are positive or negative. These affect each sibling differently, even though they were brought up in the same household. One sibling can take on responsibility, another can show love. Knowledge is an ongoing understanding of information, and we all can access it if we want.

Having faith in God has helped me through childhood, adolescence, adulthood, marriage, the birth of three children, a miscarriage, and the deaths of a sister, brother, and husband when they were young. Though I was not the apple of my parent's eye, I have lived a happy and successful life.

My motto is love heals, not time! God is Love!

I
Grandparents on Mother's Side

I will start with my grandparents on my mother's side. As a child, I did not see these grandparents very often. They lived in a very small house in Coopersville, Michigan. My mother's own father died from a farm accident when my mother was nine years old. Her mother, my grandmother, worked as a seamstress to get by. Later, grandmother married a quiet gentleman who farmed, and later they moved to the small house where I would remember them. As a child, when we visited their little house, it wasn't long after arriving when we, the grandchildren, were offered a large sugar cookie from my grandfather—a fond memory. Grandfather kept these big sugar cookies in a Maxwell House coffee can. I remember the joy it brought him, just by the glow in his face.

My grandmother had very poor health and was in a high-backed wooden wheelchair, and then later bedridden. She never, when I knew her, smiled or was a happy person. Grandmother, in fact, was very sharp to me. She died of cancer. I will never forget the smell in that small house, because forty years later when traveling with a friend who liked to stop at estate sales, I entered this small country house and was haunted by that same odor from my grandparent's house. I'm sure the owner died of cancer. My gentle, kind grandfather lived with us for his final months of life. These grandparents died in the early 1940s.

II
Grandparents on Father's Side

My father's parents were very hard workers, but had time to make my stay on their farm with my sister, Dorothy, lots of fun. They raised vegetables, chickens, pigs, grain, and had milk cows. My grandfather used horses to plow and pull the hay wagon and my grandparents made their living by farming. I loved going for overnight visits. My sister, Dorothy, and I would always go at the same time.

Our grandmother was a great cook and would bake miniature loaves of bread for us to take on picnics down by the creek. These loaves were baked in a wood stove, in gray metal and glass can covers. On their farm was a pasture where the creek ran through with beautiful rolling hills on one side. When going down to the creek, we had to watch where we stepped, because of cow dung or pie. One day, my sister and I found clay in the bank along the creek. We spent hours shaping objects and drying them on the rocks in the sun, proud of our efforts. Our grandmother would let us gather eggs, and I remember the first time removing a warm egg out of the straw nest.

We picked green- and yellow-snipped beans for dinner. Finding a small tomato in the vegetable garden and eating it with a little salt brought me great pleasure! When threshers came to help harvest the crops, which was an exciting time, my sister and I would assist with kitchen duties and set the dining room table. Grandmother made a feast consisting of mashed potatoes, gravy, beef, and pork roast, vegetables and great pies—either apple, cherry, rhubarb, or blueberry. One of the exciting things was riding high on top of the hay in the hay wagon or playing in the hayloft. I can smell the hay and grain in the bin, just writing about that time so long ago.

My bachelor uncle lived with my grandparents. He was lots of help on the farm. He also played hide-and-seek with us and tried to teach us how to hand-milk a cow. I sort of caught on but didn't like the feel of the cow's teats. My uncle would squirt milk at the barn cats from the cow's teat. The cats seem to know when it was milking time because they all came a-running for this treat, rubbing and purring all around us!

The guest sleeping quarters was upstairs at our grandparents' farmhouse. My sister and I, full of fun, would bounce on the bed. We found that wasn't the right thing to do, for the mattress and springs would come away from the frame with a loud bang! Grandmother would scold us and tell us to settle down and go to sleep, all with a loving tone in her voice.

These grandparents showed love and generosity. Plus, when they spoke in Dutch, we had it figured out they were planning to go into town for some shopping and ice cream cones for us. My grandfather always drove, I'm not sure if Grandma knew how to drive. He had a Model T Ford with shades on the back side windows. What a thrill to ride and Granddad telling along the way who lived on each farm we passed, sometimes almost going into the ditch. Yes, they were loving grandparents! A prayer was said at mealtime by my grandfather and he read from the

Bible after meals. This commitment to prayer and reading the Bible surely influenced my life.

This grandfather, my father's dad, was born in 1878, the youngest of four children. He was eleven when his father was killed by a falling tree. His mother's new husband didn't want him around. Neighbors took him in and Grandpa showed everyone how successful he was at farming. Grandpa had only gone as far as fifth grade in school but was buying carloads of binder twine for him and other farmers in the Wooster, Michigan community. Grandpa sang at funerals, developed a herd of thoroughbred Holstein cattle, sold heifers, and had a sire for use by others in the community. Also, he was the supervisor of maintenance of local township roads, which did snowplowing and road grading. His great pride and joy as a young man was the Studebaker Surrey with its patent leather dashboard, side lights with reflectors, and fringed top. This he accomplished before reaching age forty. It was recorded that his grandfather was killed by lightning while hoeing in a cornfield with his father.

My father's dad married my grandma in 1898; she had come from Germany as a child. I was fourteen when she died at age sixty-eight. My grandpa lived to see a great-grandchild. He lived his later years with his youngest son; the bachelor uncle, who married late in life. This uncle moved to the city and became a plumber. Grandpa worked part-time as a gardener before he died in 1959 at age eighty-one.

III
Father

My father was the disciplinarian and made most of the important decisions in my family. I have a difficult time writing about him. He never seemed to be able to show love, or encourage me, or praise me.

As a young man, he worked on the farm while going to school. I was told when Father was in high school, he had to read *Ben Hur* and that his mother helped him get through that book by reading some of it to him. He graduated from Fremont High School and played the cornet, which was still in my parents' belongings after my parents were both deceased. The cornet was given to my husband, a musician, to do with what he wanted. He gave it to the Blue Lake Fine Arts Museum at Twin Lake, Michigan.

My dad's first job was at Continental Motors in Muskegon, Michigan. He married and decided working for the government was a more stable job. Father started with the U.S. Postal Service as a railway mail clerk out of Detroit, Michigan. My parents moved to Detroit and lived there for a few years. His job was sorting mail on the train as it moved from town to town or city to city. Sometimes mail was put in a canvas bag on a metal arm outside the mail car. This bag was hooked by another arm at a train station where the train did not stop. His first born arrived in Detroit.

The first house my parents bought they lost in the Depression after I was born in June 1932. After renting for many years, they purchased a lot and built a new house, which was completed in March of 1941. My grandfather's farm horses dug the foundation.

The lot was ample for a big vegetable garden. Father also had strawberry plants and his famous raspberry bushes. He liked to read the Bible, but not to his children. He always said a prayer before every dinner but I can't remember how it went. It was important to him to attend church on Sunday. As he aged, the garden got smaller and grass was easier to mow now that he had a power mower. Father liked to picnic and go to a lake in the summer and, on occasion, we did go sledding with cousins in winter. My parents, however, did not go on many vacations or trips. Father did like poetry, though, especially by Edgar A. Guest. And he always drove fast. As he aged, that concerned me. I suggested he give up driving since he was getting into small accidents. He got very angry with me. My older brother came through to convince him to stop driving, as by this time, Father was in his middle eighties. His car was in the body shop so much those last few years he drove. I was very thankful for my brother's help in this matter!

As a young couple, we gave Dad the pleasure of many boat rides and went fishing with him.

After I'd remarried, my husband owned an airplane and we asked Dad if he would like a ride. It was his first and only ride in a plane. He beamed with excitement and enjoyed the ride thoroughly! Father was in his eighties. That brought back memories of riding in a small airplane in the Detroit, Michigan area when I was eight. Then my two younger brothers, being small, also went at the same time because they could fit together in one seat belt.

Friends of my parents had a brother that was the pilot. I don't know why my father didn't go that time.

The last years of my father's life were very painful. He walked with much pain. I got a wheelchair for him so we could get him out of the house for a change of scenery. Then he lost his sight. He had been treating his glaucoma for a long time it seems. He was very thin when he entered a nursing facility thirteen months before he died, in July 1990. He was ninety-one. The sad thing was I could never recall my dad showing affection to our mother or verbalizing his love to her or me.

IV
Mother

My mother was a strong person. She had to be to raise six children. She could do many things and do them well. The house was kept in good order. Of course, her children were there to help as they grew up and she made much of our clothing when we were young. She made snowsuits for my younger brothers during World War II and mending was always stacked high on the sewing machine.

Darning socks was something I learned to do. Mother could crochet and tat (tatting is a very fine trim you make and attach on collars or hankies). She was also a good cook and could and would feed big groups with ease. She also canned while I was still at home, with which I helped. Later, after I was married and living elsewhere, they bought a freezer and Mother learned to freeze different foods. She could put a wonderful dinner together and top it off with one of her delicious pies. She never had an automatic washer, dryer, or dish washer, and the home my parents lived in, they had built in 1941 and lived there until 1989, forty-eight years. Mother liked to be outside and work with her flowers. She was good with African violets, annuals, and perennial plants. She had a green thumb, definitely!

As her children grew up and married, she liked to control each one. This was not appreciated by me, and I had a difficult time maintaining a good relationship with Mother. When an accident happened or bad circumstances occurred, she would fall apart! She could not reason or think clearly in these circumstances. The first time I observed this behavior was when my youngest brother, Dean, broke his leg sliding. I was sixteen and my sister and I had to stop Mother from throwing things and hold her down in a chair. Mother, as her children left the nest, wanted to control all of her children. She started rumors that caused her children to become distant to one another. Many hardships came from this and my sisters and brothers drifted apart.

One situation when I was very proud of my mother, happened in February, 1979. At this time I was a widow and this was a first in a very serious situation. Mother, Dad, and I were invited to Dimondale, Michigan for a birthday dinner for my mother at my brother Dean's home. My brother's in-laws also lived in Grand Rapids and so he offered to drive us all to the dinner. While driving home, we were caught in a whiteout storm and the driver drove into a snowbank. We were stuck in the snow. Because the snow was blowing so hard, we could not tell what side of the road we were on. As my dad was getting out of the car, my brother's mother-in-law started to scream, "We are going to die, we are going to die!" She was also grabbing at the car's controls and the car engine was somehow turned off. Her husband tried to start it and couldn't with all this happening so fast.

For me, it was time out for a silent prayer and then to take action. I raised my voice and took control, and first found out that we were stuck on the median. After calming everyone, I told the driver to start the car, which he did. Then my dad and I got out on the left side to push the car out of the snowbank. When we were on our way again,

I suggested putting on the car's hazard lights for the rest of the way home. We arrived back in Grand Rapids safely. For her part, Mother was calm and supportive the entire time, very reassuring. She had changed.

During my first years of marriage I had a situation with my mother that really confused me as to whether I was a Christian. We bought a boat as a young family which would add to our fun at the lakes we visited and where, on occasion, we camped. Sometimes Sunday was the only day we could go. My brothers were still at home and so we would invite parents and brothers to come, too. My mother would always say no and that got to me, for we always went on picnics, even on Sundays, making sure we went to church first. So I pressed this issue with my mother and this was her answer. "You could put a picnic basket in the trunk and neighbors didn't know where you were going, but if you had a boat behind the car, that you couldn't hide."

My family through the years got together for a picnic on the Fourth of July. We celebrated our country's birthday plus my parents' wedding anniversary. On July 4, 1959 we were to meet at Muskegon State Park at the beach on Lake Michigan. My husband dropped me off to gather tables, and he went inland on Muskegon Lake to launch our boat. He would come out the channel to give boat rides and pull water skiers. I waited for a long time before he came back still towing the boat. It seems that early on the morning of the 4th of July, a pleasure cruiser was hit in the channel by Highway 16, a car carrier. Six people drowned and the Coast Guard was dragging the channel for the bodies, so no boats could come in or go out of the channel. Two people did survive. After finding out about that tragedy, we were still waiting for my parents and some other family members riding with them to arrive. We began to worry, knowing my father liked to drive fast. We later learned that Father had come upon a girl riding her bike onto the road from a driveway, and to avoid hitting her, my father had driven into a ditch. The car bounced and when it came down, my mother hit the dashboard with her chin, breaking her front teeth and cutting her lip. My brother, Dean, was in the car and said they were lucky no one else was hurt. My mother was hurting, so that day ended on a sad note.

I learned from experience and through hardships to be helpful, have patience, and stay calm.

As my mother aged, she lost control of her children. She became very tight with money and could not face change. She was taken advantage of by a slippery insurance salesman on a bogus insurance policy. Afterward, my new husband was asked to help with my parent's tax forms and realized that a supplemental policy they were paying for was worthless. We had warned Mother about this salesman, but she renewed again and then was angry with us when she didn't get her money back right away. She *did* get her money back, but it took time. This insurance man went to my parents' church—that's why they trusted him. I took the initiative to alert the church and found out that other elderly folks had had problems, too, with this same salesman. I'm sure his business stopped at that church. The church alerted their elder population of this insurance man in the church bulletin.

Mother's hygiene in later years was extinct; she could hardly take care of her own needs, so how could she help my father? She fell on the stairs many times, while helping my father up the stairs in their home. With my husband, I had taken a class on how to deal with elderly parents. When I saw they needed more help than I could give, I investigated how they could stay in their home, as was their wish. I started the ball rolling with a visiting nurse to evaluate the situation. My parents were so angry, calling me stupid (among other things), that my husband took my hand and we left their home.

I was the only sibling in the same town as my parents at that time. I let my brothers know what had happened and that's when my brother, Harold, took over. We had one meeting with three siblings agreeing upon a united front. But this never happened; picking a nursing home was decided only by my brother, Harold.

We did help by taking my father to get an exam to evaluate his health for the nursing section of the retirement home. And, I tried to help my mother organize her home before she was to move into an apartment in the same building as my father. A month later my brothers moved my mother into her apartment, Mother cursing my brothers all the way. I appreciate I didn't have to hear or see that terrible scene. I had moved to Charlevoix, Michigan. My father died thirteen months later in July 1990.

I noticed during monthly visits that my mother's care and her room were going downhill. Food service was less than desirable. I complained to my brother, Harold, several times, and he would put me off, saying it was fine. Then Mother went into assisted living and the care was even worse. When I couldn't do anything about it, my daughter with a law degree stepped in to help. First, my daughter, who on one of her visits to see her grandmother said the room smelled worse than a cat box, took her grandmother to lunch and talked to her about her care at the home, that she was *not* getting services she was paying for. Money was still important to Mother. My daughter asked her where she would like to live, if given a choice. She said right away, "Clark Home," a Methodistsupported home. My mother had been a member of the Methodist Church for many years.

My daughter and I visited Clark Home and found out what had to be done. My daughter also set up a meeting with my brother, Harold, who agreed to the move after much protesting. My mother had to be evaluated again for proper placement in her new home.

The day of her move, my husband and I were to take her to lunch. Brothers Harold and Dean would move her furniture and clothes. When we got to Mother's room, it smelled very bad. She was in such disorder! She had no undergarments on, no Depends, only a cotton housedress and shoes without any pantyhose or socks. Her hair looked like it hadn't been washed in weeks. After washing her up, getting proper clothes, and fixing her hair the best I could, we were off to lunch and then to her new home. We were immediately introduced to the staff on Mother's floor and a nurse, noting mother's hair, said, "I will get a hair appointment for you in the morning." Mother's new home was a new concept in nursing care, called households. Her room was off a large, pleasant room that had a TV, couch, round tables for meals, and a piano to share. It was a great place for family to visit. Eight private bedrooms big enough for a dresser, desk, end table, comfortable chair, toilet room, bed, and large closet were off of the main room. Many opportunities were offered to Mother. She did have a difficult time, however, adjusting to her new home; she was over ninety now. But visiting at this home was very nice and Mother was always clean and properly dressed. What a blessing!

In June of 1997, on a Saturday, we were in Grand Rapids for my husband's fiftieth class reunion. He was helping with the program so I had a few hours to spend with my mother. I brought my clipboard and wrote everything down so she would understand everything I said as her hearing aids didn't always work. We had a good visit; she seemed to appreciate me so much since I'd moved away.

Once, my brother and his wife brought Mother partway up north and we took her on up to our new home. She loved being in the woods. The next time Mother visited for a few days we took her for a boat ride. We lived on a lake, and at ninety-three she was so pleased! When getting ready to take her back home, she cried. Maybe she knew it would be her last visit.

So back to that Saturday in June 1997. Having sort of straightened her room, I wished her good-bye. The following Monday, my husband took the call that Mother had experienced a heart problem and had been brought to the hospital then released. Because I had just been with her, I decided to wait and see how she did over the next couple of days. She died two days later, on Wednesday. Mother was ninety-five and had eleven grandchildren, eleven great-grandchildren, and one great-great-grandchild.

My husband came up with a saying about my mother's two retirement homes: She went from the outhouse to the penthouse.

One thing, very interesting, was that my mother could never say she loved me. When I asked her in later years if she loved me, she said she just couldn't say "I love you." Don't get me wrong, my mother did have some good qualities, but low self-esteem.

I was in shock, as well as my children, at my mother's memorial service. A grandchild got up immediately and came forward when the minister asked if anyone had comments they would like to share. I never knew of the tender and loving relationship between this grandchild and my mother.

I then got up and read my poem, titled "Just Her Little Girl." This came about because this is how my mother would introduce me to her friends.

Mother showed many ways to live life
Good and bad, not without strife
Important to be proper and look your best
God is watching and gives his test
Rewards are abundant, but not all at once
Mother knew they could come in a bunch
For around that corner is another blessing
She's at peace with the Lord, her family caressing!

My youngest brother was the last to speak. He told of his mother's many accomplishments: gardening, cooking, canning, freezing foods, and her many sewing projects. This brother was proud to tell his fellow students, when walking in the school's hall, that the wonderful smell of roast beef cooking was his mother fixing the meal for the P.T.A. dinner.

I did forget to tell you at my father's service the minister did not suggest comments from family or friends.

V
First Born

My sister, Laura, was the first born in our family in the year 1923. My parents were living in Detroit, Michigan at that time. When sorting through pictures after our parents were gone, pictures of her out-numbered the rest of us ten to one. That, of course, is not unusual in families. Laura was given piano lessons, my parents purchased a Baldwin piano and later got an accordion for her, which I remember her playing, but never heard her play the piano. There were no music lessons for the rest of us kids.

Telling you about my sister is a sad tale. We are nine years apart in age. There are three happenings, well, maybe four, that I can clearly remember of this sister when I was young. The first was when I was around six years old. I was playing Mother May I on my friends' and neighbors' concrete steps. I had a bad fall and opened my head on the corner of a step. I was bleeding profusely. My sister was at home and came to get me after being called by the neighbor. Laura cleaned me up and took care of my clothes. This sister comforted me when my parents were not home to help. I can still feel the slight ridge on my forehead, and can see a small scar.

The second memory was when I was a big tease and threw a glass of water out the upstairs window when my sister's boyfriend brought her up to the front door after date.

The third memory was when I made the cheerleading team in junior high. My sister was married and living out of state but had come home for a visit. She thought it was time to cut my braids, so my sister cut and styled my hair, which made me very happy!

The fourth memory was her explaining I wasn't bleeding to death when I got my period. When she got married, I was not happy about her choice of mate. However, I was young and what did I know!

My life was changing. Marriage, having a baby, and finding my way as a young mother took a turn I didn't expect. My sister never acknowledged when my children were born, never held them in her arms. We had little communication and I would only see her at family functions. Then our sister, Dorothy, was diagnosed with cancer and died within the year. My older sister never visited her and did not come to her younger sister's funeral. Her reason was that doctors made up cancer as a way to make money.

I had a very hard time with my sister being so hard-hearted. Was she so unhappy, what was going on with her life?

I was about thirty when I got a letter from this sister's husband asking me to have lunch with him. He was coming into town for a conference. I thought this would give me a chance to open communications again with my sister, his wife. My husband said go for it, since I didn't get out to lunch that often. I was to meet him at a restaurant and he suggested we have a drink first, so we did. Then, to my surprise, he said he didn't have time for lunch, but had to show me something he had in his hotel room. I was very naive. There was nothing to show me—he wanted an affair. I was upset and didn't care if I ever saw him again. Letters began to come from him asking me not to tell anyone . . . how ludicrous! At that time, the only persons who knew were my husband and my youngest brother, whom I was very close to at the time. My sister never knew, that I'm aware of, according to a statement she made to me in June 2004 when we saw each other after many years. She trusted her husband implicitly.

Laura and her husband had a very conservative lifestyle. They had a nice home and a garden of irises. Laura even went as far as learning to hybridize to get new species of irises. They never had children. Visits with family were rare. Even getting Laura and her husband to come to holiday celebrations, picnics, or her nieces' or nephews' weddings was something she did not care about. Laura and her husband received wedding invitations to all her siblings' weddings, but only showed up at her younger brother, Bob's. Actually, the ceremony was over and people had begun to leave the reception when they came. I began to wonder if Laura was a prisoner in her own home. I never, to this day, knew what motivated her.

Nineteen years after my sister died, my younger brother was dying of cancer. My sister, Laura, and her husband were interested in my brother, Bob, who also had a diagnosis of cancer. My brother was having lots of back pain. My sister's husband, a chiropractor, thought he could relieve some of the pain for my brother, which helped very little. My brother died at age thirty-four. I did not know that Bob was quite close to his older sister when Bob attended Michigan State. I only found out this connection after Bob's death. Laura and her husband did come to Brother Bob's funeral.

Laura was a new widow when our father died, and she came to our father's funeral. She lived in Pennsylvania at that time. Her husband had his roots in Pennsylvania and wanted to move there when he retired. It was not a happy time for them because of my sister's husband's failing health. He died soon after settling into their new home. Laura then moved back to Lansing, Michigan where she had friends. When Mother died, Laura lived in Lansing, but didn't come to her mother's funeral. She didn't want to associate with her siblings. She has ridiculed me at gatherings. After being propositioned by her husband in person and in letters, I withdrew from her, not knowing what else to do. When my son's first wife asked for a list of guests we would like to attend their wedding, and we were limited, we gave her a list. I did not include Laura and her husband because Laura never showed any interest in any of my children. To my surprise, my mother said she would not come if we didn't invite Laura and her husband. So an invitation was sent. The results were bad! Laura wrote a nasty letter to the bride-to-be's parents explaining, that my husband and I were not fit parents and their daughter would be marrying below her. I was very upset. My late husband got the letter before the wedding from the bride-to-be's father. My late husband gave it to me to read on our way home from the wedding reception and I brought the letter directly for my mother and father to read, but I was just blown off! Were we Christians?

I made a study of sibling rivalry and tried to understand why my sister was the way she was. I even sent her the articles. She informed me that she knew all there was to know about sibling rivalry. I thought it was possibly because she had to take care of her younger siblings.

One day out of the blue I got a call at work from my sister, wondering how I was. I had just found out my late husband had cancer and there wasn't much hope for him. She, my sister, seemed to be interested and compassionate and wanted to stay in touch. This was so different for her. When she called at work again, I was on a leave of absence. She was told my husband was in the hospital. She and her husband came to see my husband, so I had to explain to my dying husband how she had come into my life again. He would see them, but cautioned me to be careful.

After my husband died, Laura seemed to be pleasant and we did go to dinner and visited at each of our homes a few times. When my daughter, who was in college, suggested we have a weekend with just the girls, Laura's husband ended our friendship. He would not allow her to be with us.

When I met the man I would marry and brought him to meet my family at a Christmas gathering, I was upset at how my sister and her husband degraded my future mate. Again the abusive letters came. Again my prayer life went into high gear.

September 12, 1994 was the first and last wedding my sister, Laura, would attend. Getting married was our niece, my late Brother Bob's, daughter. I was very cautious. My instincts told me if she approached me, greet her. But she stayed away from me.

After both our parents had died, I sent Laura letters asking her if she would like any keepsakes of our parents. I sent her all of the photos that would be of interest to her. She never acknowledged. When I started to gather material for this book, I sent out a questionnaire to all my siblings in February 2002. I wanted some verification of where she was born and any memories she would like to share. She didn't answer. I have written the book without questions answered from this sister.

In early November 2002, a long-time prayer of mine was finally answered. I received a letter from Laura agreeing to meet me for lunch. I was so happy I told my brothers, who thought I was crazy. The reunion was on

November 14, 2002 and was great! We hugged! There was lots to cover and with tears and forgiveness, all went very well. She even brought a small gift for me.

Remember, I am the peacemaker. We are all blessed with God's Grace but sometimes don't realize it. Prayer to me is bringing God's Grace to fruition! It was only a few visits and an overnight stay at my home, in June 2003. After that stay, however, she would not answer any of my letters and would hang up when I called her.

I realized my sister's memory was very bad. She was getting lost when traveling out of town. Some memories would come back when I showed her pictures. She said she did not read much and that worried me. She couldn't tell me why she had treated her family so badly. What will become of her? My prayers for her are continuing! Is she lost forever? Does she have Alzheimer's disease?

VI
Second Born

My brother, Harold, was the first-born son in the year 1927, and to my parents, their pride and joy. He was born in an upstairs rented apartment in Southwest Grand Rapids, Michigan. Harold was a fair student and loved playing football in high school. When I was having a hard time with algebra and he was in college, he helped me and I got through that class just fine.

Before college, Harold served his years in the army in Los Alamos, New Mexico as an MP. He was there during an explosion when some men were exposed to radiation, something my family didn't seem to know much about or understand at that time. After the service, he went to college on the GI Bill. In college he took engineering and graduated as a civil engineer from Michigan State University, after which he took a job with the Highway Department in California. I'm not sure why.

At that time I was a busy young mother. Harold was engaged, and the first Christmas in California his betrothed came out to be with him for Christmas (the trip was a present from her parents) only to give him back the engagement ring and call off the engagement. He then came back to Michigan, possibly to patch things up, which never happened. Harold then went to work for the Michigan Highway Department as a bridge engineer.

Around that time, my parents, with my two younger brothers, joined a large downtown Methodist church. Harold would go to the same church while in town and that is where met his wife. Harold had dated a few girls and my late husband and I would invite them to dinner. He soon announced his engagement to Carol and a wedding date was set. Carol, my sister-in-law-to-be, asked me to be a bridesmaid, but I would've been eight months pregnant on the wedding date, so instead my late husband and I were the mistress and master of ceremonies, which was an honor. We got to know the bride's parents very well.

Harold was the first in our family to marry and have a church wedding. Mother felt very insecure about everything, but put on a wonderful rehearsal dinner for Harold in the family home. Harold said his best decision was to marry Carol. Another joy in his life are his three children and seven grandchildren; these were answers from the questionnaire I sent to each surviving sibling.

God is important in Harold's life, and the person who influenced him the most was his mother. The best thing that happened to him as a child was falling into Lake Macatawa in Holland, Michigan when boarding a motor launch to tour the lake. Harold was around five or six years old when this happened. It could have been tragic, but he was rescued. After a few years in engineering he decided to go to seminary to become a Methodist minister but he never shared why he made that decision. Still, Harold had a very hard time with his studies when in seminary, for it was around the time his sister was ill. Dorothy passed away in a very short time. Nineteen years later his brother, Bob, died. Harold discovered life was very fragile.

Harold's favorite memory as a teenager was fishing

as a team on Big Star lake in northern Michigan. Standing in the water with some kids with long cane poles they would fish, and when they caught a fish, the kids on shore would take them off and put the new bait back on the hook. The most important memento left by his parents were bookends they kept for many years. Harold had made them in a class while at Michigan State. After being a minister for a time, he became a city engineer and worked for a private contractor. He also went back to the Michigan State Highway Department when he retired, and then worked a short time for the city of Belding, Michigan. Harold didn't want me to help finding a retirement home for my parents; I gave suggestions from reliable connections all to no avail. Harold is very secretive about many things, as was his mother, and we have not had good communication through the years. Before he had to deal with my parents, he called *me* paranoid about my parents. I had been the one caregiver when things were going downhill with my parents. To his credit, Harold, as well as my husband, did work on our parents' house when repairs were needed.

Harold also had power-of-attorney for my parents. I think he understood my predicament after being the primary caregiver to our mother for almost eight years. He even admitted Mother was devious through much of her life. When taking care of my parents' Trust, Harold again became secretive. After I requested a copy of the Trust, I saw the instructions to the Trust stated that all those named in the Trust should have a copy. He finally did come through with a copy of the Trust, but very reluctantly. Harold also said he took my parents to their lawyer to make some changes Harold thought necessary. Harold has never been open about these facts with me. Communication is still marginal.

The author's grandparents on her mother's side, 1914

The wedding picture of the author's grandparents

on her father's side, circa 1897

The author's parents in 1938

The author and all of her siblings in 1942

The author's birthplace. Her parents lost this house during the Depression, 1932.

Dressed in her green snowsuit, the author pushes her youngest brother in a Campbell's tomato juice box, 1938.

The author poses with her sister, just four years her senior, outside one of the houses their family rented.

The author and her first love

Peeking out next to the teacher while posing with her Sunday school class

Built by the author's parents in 1941, the family lived here for forty-eight years.

The author's youngest brother—her children's favorite uncle

Picture taken in Chicago, on our honeymoon May 13, 1951

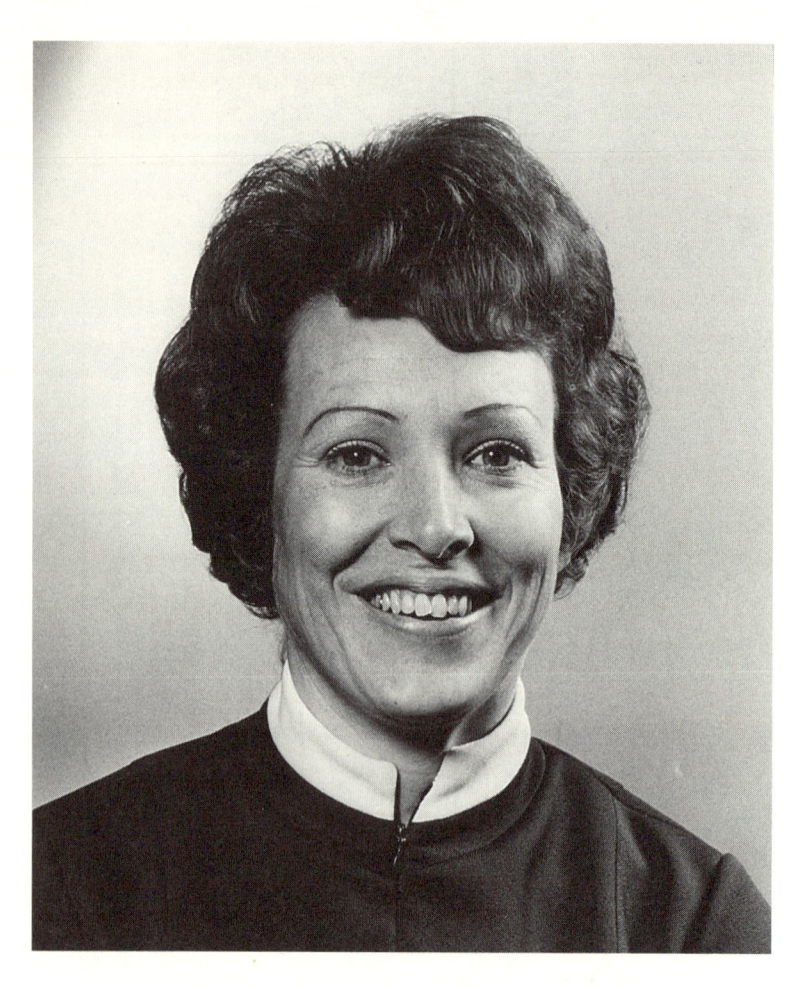

First president of Creston High School's booster club for women's sports

The author as a widow in 1980

Meeting President Ford and Michigan's Governor Milliken to thank them for their help with her late husband's place of business

The author's second wedding day, March 5, 1983

Meeting the champ, Ali, at O'Hare Airport in 1994

VII
Third Born

My sister, Dorothy, was the third child born in the year 1928, less than two years after Harold, in the same upstairs apartment in southwest Grand Rapids, Michigan. Then the family moved to a nicer area and rented a home. Not too long after, another move to yet another rented home, but close to the school we would all attend.

Dorothy was a rather shy child, although she did play with the neighborhood children. This group of kids had many activities together; one was to play Kick the Can. I was responsible for chipping Dorothy's front tooth, when I kicked the can and it somehow hit my sister. My parents never took her to the dentist to have it capped.

Dorothy and I were in Youth Group at church together. We went on picnics and played softball. Dorothy was a good athlete. Her first date, brother Harold made for her. Then after high school graduation she worked part-time and went to Kendall School of Design in Grand Rapids, Michigan.

Dorothy was very artistic. She shared her clothes with me, if I would press them or do her hand wash and polish her shoes regularly. When I got married in May of my senior year of high school, Dorothy wanted so much to marry too, but hadn't known her young man for very long. I wasn't in a position to give advice, but my late husband,

and my brother, Harold, thought this person a loser and let her know. Yet she jumped into marriage, a life which turned bad from the start. Her husband threatened her, and went regularly to bars to drink. She became pregnant soon after the wedding, but her husband couldn't seem to keep a job. Dorothy was changing and seemed to think everyone owed her a living. I felt she was jealous of me and that made our relationship harder to keep. Her baby came, but it was a difficult delivery.

My parents made Dorothy go to their doctor, who was an osteopath. When I had my third child, Dorothy had been wanting another baby, so I suggested she go to a gynecologist and gave her my doctor's name. Dorothy's husband was still changing jobs almost every month, and when Dorothy called to say they were moving to Kalamazoo, Michigan, and that her father-in-law was setting up a silk screening business for his son, I was thinking how wonderful, because of Dorothy's artistic talent. Before moving to Kalamazoo, however, I knew she was having health problems since she had to have all her teeth pulled and got a full set of dentures. Then, after moving, something else was wrong. Dorothy had a mastectomy and doctors were not sure they got all the cancer. That was in the spring.

Dorothy seemed to improve over the summer, but in September started going downhill. On her deathbed she told me she had gone to my doctor more than two years ago, but nothing more. I checked with my doctor on my next yearly appointment, asking him if my sister had had an appointment with him. His nurse pulled Dorothy's file and the doctor told me to come to his office after I got dressed. While reading her file, the doctor shook his head and said it can't be my sister. She was so depressed about her marriage, wanted another child, but when a lump was found in her breast, she passed up the option of getting a second opinion and to have a biopsy done right away! The time span from that time to her move to Kalamazoo to her mastectomy was a little over two years. During that time, the cancer had spread. Would she still be alive if she had taken care of it right away?

Dorothy died the day before her thirty-second birthday, October 13, 1960. My mother was grief-stricken and somehow alienated her son-in-law so that he withdrew from our family with his daughter, who was nine years old. We did not see him or my niece for several years. This brother-in-law of mine died in his middle fifties.

VIII
Fourth Born and Author of This Book.

Shirley, that's me, was the fourth-born child, arriving in the year 1932. We lived on North Monroe, in Grand Rapids, Michigan. My parents were buying their first home, which they lost in the Depression. Mother told everyone she was carrying a boy. After I was born, Mother did not believe I was a girl, so she took off my diaper to check, while under twilight sleep. This is something given to women in labor, years ago. She was disappointed I was a girl. Mother wanted two girls and two boys.

Our family did grow with the births of two brothers, which later made it three girls and three boys.

My first recollection was when I was around four years old. I think having photos of the occasion helps the memory. Our family had rented a cottage at Big Star Lake in Michigan and I had made friends with a boy from Chicago. We made sand castles, rivers, and lakes on the beach and we both loved splashing in the water. My first girlfriend was Helen, who lived a couple of houses away. It was on Helen's back steps where I fell and suffered a bad head wound. She was a year younger than me, and when she got a two-wheel bike for her fifth birthday, I learned to ride it first.

We had lots of fun playing Hide and Seek, jumping

off the garage into a big Forsythia bush, and climbing trees. When I started school, the first two years were very difficult for me. Then, in second grade, my teacher helped me so much that learning became a big adventure. This teacher introduced me to birds (which even today I find fascinating), how to organize, do things to help others, and being a dependable friend. This teacher is still living today, 2005. In the summer of 2000, I spent lunch and a boat ride with her, her husband, my husband, and mutual friends. She (my second grade teacher) asked my husband if I was an organized person. He was amazed when my teacher told him how I helped find things in the cupboards for many projects in the classroom. Mrs. Betty Rosendall was a great influence in my life.

My fourth grade teacher, Mrs. Thelma Key, I liked as well. These teachers showed kindness. Mrs. Key taught us to knit and she put the squares her students knitted into an afghan for wounded soldiers in World War II. Once, I was spanked by her, but I don't remember why. I still thought she was a good teacher.

In the fourth grade, my mother decided to let my hair grow and put it in pigtails. Every morning until eighth grade, Mother braided my long hair which, before it was cut, was so long I could sit on it when it was hanging loose. In fifth grade, Mother said I could have a birthday party so I invited a few girls and my teacher, Mrs. Lymburner. It was a year after D-Day, June 6, 1944, a day to remember.

I also wanted to take piano lessons since we had a beautiful Baldwin piano that no one in our family played. Sometimes, when we had company, the company would play. My parents said no and that was final! I never had my own bike like my siblings, and when I was old enough to drive, my father would never let me or even show me how to drive. So, the boys I dated taught me, and I drove one of their cars for my test drive.

When I started junior high, one morning I woke up frightened when I saw blood all over my p.j.s and the bed sheet. I thought I was dying. My older sister, Laura, was visiting and explained, which was very helpful. My older brother really embarrassed me when I came downstairs by saying, "I hear you're a young lady now."

I began to go with boys to school dances and the movies. In eighth grade I made the cheerleading team and got to go on the bus with the boys' basketball team to all the basketball games. I was a cheerleader for three years. In the spring, as a teenager, I got jobs cleaning out leaves in neighbors' shrubs and mowed lawns in the summer. It was very hard to get money for extras from my parents. By tenth grade I was buying most of my own clothes and school supplies. I also had lots of babysitting jobs. However, I cannot remember my parents encouraging me in any of my endeavors.

In ninth grade I had a fling with a young man who was at the University of Michigan in Ann Arbor. He was a nephew of people for whom I babysat. Then I started dating Dave; I'd known him since fifth grade. I did go out with different young men until my senior year, but then Dave became a steady date and we talked of getting married. He had graduated the year before and had a job. I didn't plan on going to college because I couldn't see how I could finance it, and my parents were unwilling to help.

In my senior year I learned how to be a long distance operator and enjoyed the work. Dave became very special to me although his home life was not good. His father was an alcoholic as well as his stepmother, and I felt sad about this. We were seeing each other every day and Dave would pick me up from work when he could. The romance developed with all our love shared with each other. We began to look forward to my graduation and getting married. Then I got pregnant, but was still able to graduate. I talked with the student counselor and we worked everything out at school, but home was a different story. My parents were very upset with me. I was humiliated to the point of being shaken by my father, who knocked me down the stairs when I tried to get away from him. The trauma was unbelievable. First, my parents wanted to know if it was true, and that I go to their doctor. This doctor suggested an abortion. I said no. Then they wanted me to go to my brother-in-law, a chiropractor, whom I did not like or trust. Talk about humiliating experiences; this was a capital one!

I was in such turmoil from my parents and Dave took their harassment too. He tried hard to calm them, even coming up with a plan. He suggested we go to his cousin, who was a prominent gynecologist in our city. Dave and I went together, with no parents to interfere. This doctor was a wonderful, compassionate person! He asked us if we loved each other, looking directly at us, we said "Yes!" His remark was, "Then why don't you get married?" When I look back, that is what we wanted, but my parents were tearing us apart. This cousin delivered our first-born, a son.

Dave and I were married six months before our son was born. The wedding was very simple, and was held at my parent's home. Both of our parents attended, as well as my brothers and the minister and his wife. My parents knew a retired minister who came with his wife to marry us. No wedding cake or trimmings. We flew to Chicago for a weekend honeymoon. I wore a navy suit with a small white linen hat and Dave wore a gray suit. This was the beginning of a happy union of two people who deeply cared for each other.

Our first decision as a married couple was to find a place to live. My parents were generous enough to let us stay with them until the baby came. It helped us out, because we had just enough saved to pay for the doctor and hospital bills. After our son was born, we started looking for an apartment. My parents were checking us out on every apartment we would pick, and they always disapproved. It was hard to break away, but finally we moved. We were also looking for a church in which we could raise our child. When I was breastfeeding our son on Sunday mornings, we listened to a minister on the radio and Dave said he liked his messages, so we decided to join the church of the radio minister. Dave was brought up Catholic so I was very happy with his decision. To our surprise, my parents, with my younger brothers, wanted to join too. On February 24, 1952, we as a couple, our son, my parents, and Bob and Dean, my brothers, joined the Methodist church. My late husband and I took an active part in the church, but in later years, we got a new minister who was so disappointing to us that we dropped off our attendance. About that time, my parents took an interest in the church's senior group, which had monthly luncheons.

Activities increased with our children in sports and music. We purchased our first boat in the late 1950s. As our children got old enough, each one learned to water ski and we purchased a bigger boat as the family grew in size. Dave and I were taught first, to water ski, by our boating friends. As a family, we camped almost every weekend in the summer and all over Michigan on summer vacations. Michigan has some of the most beautiful state parks in the United States. We encouraged our son to continue with his education after high school, but he had a good job and did not want to go to college. Karen, our second child, did go to a junior college, but did not do well. We suggested she do better or find a job—so she found a job. Kathy, our youngest, was a senior when Dave, my late husband, was diagnosed with cancer. We got the bad news in the middle of October 1977; he died March 2, 1978.

Dave was in the hospital for six weeks and I took a leave of absence from work to be with him. Each day I would bathe him and sometimes take him to the radiation department. His cancer spread so fast that all parts of his body were shutting down. We talked when he couldn't sleep. Dave struggled, but was failing fast, and we were both looking for answers. About eight days before Dave died, a priest came (don't know how or why) and inquired if Dave would like to see and talk with him. Dave went to Catholic school until sixth grade. I asked Dave and he said yes, and I left the room. After the priest came out of Dave's room, I thanked him and went back in. It was the first time in months I saw Dave at peace. I was so thankful! Looking back, I think the priest gave Dave the last rites.

A week later, Dave went into a coma, a few days before dying. On March 2, 1978, a Friday morning, I was to check in at Dave's place of employment to see if I could get any sick pay. It had been about six weeks with no money coming in. I would do this before going to the hospital to be with Dave. Dave had been in a coma for two days, and the nurse said he could hear me speak, but could not answer. That was very hard for me, to see him in that state.

My daughter, Kathy, was home from college with the flu when I drove home first for some papers. I could see her sitting in a chair and wondered why she was out of bed. She said the hospital called and wanted me to come right away.

Dave had died about half an hour before I arrived, the nurse in his room told me, and then gave me a hug. She asked if I wanted his wedding ring, to which I said yes, and she took it off his finger. She left me alone with him for a short time as I got my thoughts together. Putting my hand on his, I said, "Good-bye, my love and father of our beautiful children!" It was so still in the room, at first I thought I saw my late husband move. Then I left to call my son and my youngest brother. I hadn't seen my parents for five years, at this time, because my mother had treated Dave with disrespect too many times. Then my parents got word, from my brother, Harold, that Dave was dying. Dave did not want to see them, and that decision I could understand. Visitors were screened toward the last days of Dave's life.

Dave had a half-sister who was about eleven years younger and who we would see occasionally. We did not approve of her live-in, sometimes, boyfriend. One day, his half-sister called to say she was coming to visit and asked if I needed anything. It so happened to be that I did need a ride home from the hospital as my daughter needed the car. Dave's half-sister said she and her boyfriend would like to take me to dinner after they visited my dying husband. Well, as it turned out, only the boyfriend turned up at the hospital. I wasn't happy about that so I turned down dinner, and it was hard to convince him when he took me home that I did not want him to come into my house. Well, it's unbelievable what rumors Dave's half-sister started. She told anyone who would listen that I had taken her boyfriend away from her, a man who I did not even like or trust! I have not seen her since her mother's funeral in 1981.

When her mother had a stroke and was in the hospital, she did not let me know. I found out from her mother's friend. When I went to see her, my late husband's stepmother was so happy to see us. She was laying in her hospital bed, and when my daughter and her fiancé also came for a visit at the hospital, I'm sure by her actions that she knew her daughter had not told us. Her speech came very hard, but her loving smile to us was welcoming. She passed away soon after our visit, a sad situation for a lady who could write such a wonderful love story for me about her stepson. A few years later the boyfriend of the half-sister had moved out west and had committed suicide by jumping off a bridge.

After I left Dave at the hospital, I went to see a funeral director. Dave and I had agreed we both wanted to be cremated. I knew an undertaker who belonged to our church so on my way home I stopped at his establishment. The owners were on vacation and a young man was on duty so I told him what I wanted: that my husband's body was to be cremated and at which cemetery he was to be buried. Then, how I wanted the obituary to read. The young man proceeded to tell me that my request was all wrong, and that I could not put what I wanted in the obituary even when I had to pay. I was, of course, upset, took a breath, and convinced him that that was how I wanted things. He finally agreed. Because of a request from my younger brother, Dean, no autopsy or taking of parts for transplants was to take place. When I got home, my son was there, very worried as to where I had been. The hospital staff had told him I was on my way home as I did not tell them I was stopping at the funeral home first. I told my son what I had planned—to open our home for friends and family to give their condolences. He seemed to think that was fine.

Following is a tribute I wrote years later, just before one Memorial Day. I was somehow called to do this written tribute to the man from whom I learned so much, and who had helped me grow in my faith. Years later, I read that it is very therapeutic to write down the memories of a loved one.

A clear reminder of this wonderful person:

A Tribute to Dave

For you who never had the opportunity to know him and for those who have forgotten his legacy, this we remember.

Dave was born in Grand Rapids on July 21, 1932 to Ella and Fred Schuitema. His parents had gone through the Great Depression without considerable financial loss, but by the time Dave was four years old, life for this young boy became very difficult. His mother died of cancer and his father become an alcoholic. Rumors from relatives were blaming Dave for her death. He had little support or love. As he grew, he went out for sports, but his family never took the time to share in his activities. His stepmother was treated as little more than a servant in the house, and she soon let alcohol rule her life. Dave was raised a Catholic and went to parochial school until the sixth grade. This is when I first met him. He graduated from high school the year before I did, and we married the year I graduated. When our first child came along, Dave dropped out of the Naval Reserves, because he wanted to be a full-time father.

As a young dad, he wanted his children brought up in the church. Our background of faith came from the United Methodist church. I remember those early years with Dave as being a time when my life was first being filled with joy. Dave seemed to turn darkness into light, dreams into real-

ity. I never had a bike as a child; he bought me one. As a family we camped and went boating, so we all learned to water ski with Dave guiding the way patiently.

Dave worked hard at all he did. He was a typographer by trade and was in a union for eighteen years. He saw much plundering in the union and wouldn't tolerate it. When the shop went out on strike, he walked across picket lines at the shop where he worked and rallied enough workers to keep the place open, thus forming a nonunion shop. His children remember the threats over the phone, at all hours, and the vandalism of our home. Through this period of time we all saw his courage. As our children grew he was there; watching them in sports, helping in activities and encouraging them to go to college. He did live to see his son married, but never the joys of grandchildren or of seeing his youngest graduate from high school with honors and go to college. Dave died on March 2, 1978, a victim of cancer.

I give Dave much praise for helping me develop the faith and courage to carry on and live with Dick, who understands and is very complimentary of Dave, knowing how he influenced the person I am and the way I live.

I am able to write this because of a healing of time. Memorial Day is just past, and it is a time when we remember loved ones who have gone on before us. My memories of Dave are filled with gratitude for a husband and father that had so much love in his heart. He taught me about the freedom that comes with responsibility. Thank you and God bless you, my Dave.

Epilogue: *Dave would be proud to know today that his son Tom is successful in his job, even while his employer is scaling down. His daughter Karen is single, has a good job and is currently buying a home. Kathy, the youngest, married after college. When her husband began his medical residency, she started law school. She had two sons during the time, finished in four years and passed the* *bar exams as well. She and her husband now have a third son.*

Dave's gift to his children is a strong work ethic and a sense of pride in oneself!

Dave was cremated, as was his wish. I received many sympathy cards, donations to the Cancer Society in memory of David, and a few flower arrangements were sent to my home. One day, my mother-in-law came to help me write the "Thank You" notes. Just before leaving, she handed me an envelope, and said to read it after she left. This is what she wrote about my late husband and I.

While "Love Story" was sweeping through the reading public, there was one being lived superior to this fiction in scope for its beginning was the high school sweethearts through the birth and rearing of their children.

David had a cruel and lonely childhood. When he met Shirley he began a new and meaningful life in which he walked with pride and love.

At nineteen they had their first child, Tom. Then came Karen and Kathy. The home became the center of their being.

Shirley and David were like youngsters enjoying the sports and school activities of their children. But, wise in the knowledge that children must be led to choose the right path. The five of them learned together from this ever-present training. They were set free to use their natural abilities to the fullest. Each in their own way have become very special people. The children are going out in the world after years spent in a loving and steadfast home. They have the strong guard of discipline to keep them from most temptations and to turn them to the pursuit of a fulfilling life. Their lives were enriched by Shirley's giving David a brother and sister—Dean and Louise—with whom they shared so much. And, their empathy of others which gave them the ability to make true and lasting friendships—one of the finest gifts of life.

By careful budgeting and wise spending they were able to purchase a home in a good school district. Hard work in off duty hours made it a beautiful place. Finally they could move into a house in a park-like neighborhood, much redecorating and yard work made it distinctly theirs.

There are two moments I shall always remember for they reflected the love of two people. Shirley was standing at the kitchen counter of their first home. She was totally absorbed in the cutting of a pie she had made. She placed the first piece aside and said, "This is for Dave's lunch." The second occurred when David was sitting on the edge of a hospital bed—restless in his agony. Shirley sat down next to him, put her arms around him, snuggled her head close to his, and talking low comforted him. While sitting in the hospital room I tried to escape from the knowledge that soon the ones David loved so much would be plunged into grief. The waves of which would engulf them, pulling them under until they would be "as a voice crying in the wilderness" releasing for a while to let them be a part of the everyday world, only to return and crush again.

I firmly believe David's purpose in life was completed the morning of Friday, March the second. He, then received, "Well done my good and faithful servant" and entered into everlasting happiness and the "peace that passeth all understanding."

This beautiful story (letter) to me was so uplifting and sincere from a mother-in-law that had such a hard life of her own. I send her blessings wherever she is today and "thanks for being you!"

The next letter was from a friend, and these were the only two handwritten notes I received.

Dear Shirley,

When I read of David's death in the paper, I was remiss in not coming to see you at that time, call it lack of courage on my part. In times like this it is hard to audibly express one's true concern. Perhaps now I can convey in a letter what has been on my mind the past week.

The scourge of cancer has struck you twice, first the death of your brother and now with David. There is no reasoning to this untimely suffering and loss.

In retrospect I guess we have to feel it isn't the quantity of life but the quality of life that counts.

David had many of the good things in life. A man is judged by his ability to work and support his family. David did all this plus he gave them the luxury of a warm summer day boating and water skiing. He provided them with a secure home and environment to mature in.

He has a wife who is not only attractive and attentive; she has the quality of being a loving partner and an excellent and compassionate mother.

The end results of your fine children speak well of David as a father and man, and of you as a helpmate and mother.

I know nothing can compensate for your loss, but I want you to know of my concerns and love for you at this dark time in your life.

Hold the moments close to your heart of the good times in life with David. Perhaps it will help ease the sad and discouraging time.

Loving concerns from your friend,
Elaine Youngs

Elaine did not know I had also lost a sister to cancer. These two correspondences have helped me express myself through the years. Yes, it does take courage. Thanks, Elaine!

I went back to work after being gone for six weeks.

My friends would come up to me to talk and quite often we would both be in tears. Those times soon passed. I had much to do, keeping the house up, getting the roof re-shingled and the kitchen remodeled.

I would live in that house until Kathy got married, as I had promised her. The insurance money helped make payments and do what was necessary to help sell the house. My income would not be enough to maintain the house for too long. I thought my middle daughter might want to come home and live with me. She was struggling with her finances so I thought we could help each other. I wasn't aware of the change in her lifestyle. It seems her basketball coach at college was having lots of parties and some involved sleepovers, which Karen enjoyed. Karen even tried to convince me this was a great lifestyle and for me to become one of the party group. She was very irresponsible when she moved in with me, and I couldn't put up with her not letting me know when she would be home for meals or if she would come home at all. Two weeks later I said I couldn't take her lack of being considerate, so she moved out. We also saw a therapist for a couple of sessions, which seemed to make things worse!

One day, after that calamity and still grieving and lonely, missing the life I once had, I opened my mail to read a very threatening letter addressed to me and my youngest daughter, Kathy. I was reading it when a good friend rang my doorbell. She asked, "Is something wrong?" when I opened the door, as my face was white with fright. I had experienced some vandalism of my yard, had a stone thrown through my front window, and dealt with a window peeper, but this was really scary! I went to the police department and was directed to a detective to whom I gave the letter. He instructed me that if another letter looking similar comes, do not open it, because the letter would have fingerprints. Then try to remember, in the meantime, anyone acting different toward me. That was sort of a laugh because just becoming a widow, everyone, friends and family alike, treated me different. But now I was more careful about thinking who could do something so bad to hurt both my daughter and I.

At my work, a young man who had dated Kathy would not speak to me since he was upset that my daughter was dating other college students and making new friends at college. I notified the detective about this person and gave him his name. This young man was the culprit as fingerprints verified. Would I be pressing charges? I asked only that the young man be counseled and made to understand the pain he caused and that what he did was very wrong!

What would I have to endure next?

Still seeking a way to help meet expenses, I was asked by a friend at work if I would consider a boarder. This younger woman who wanted to board would turn out to be a disaster. I am an orderly person and she was not, so I had to ask her to leave, which was very difficult for me. About a month had gone by when I was approached again about a boarder. This time, having had experience, I made a list of rules. This young woman was getting her teaching degree soon and would be practice teaching at a school in my neighborhood. She was such a blessing! She helped by cutting our grocery bill (her father owned a grocery store) and she brought a cooler filled with frozen meats. This young woman was like having a loving daughter. She was living with me when I had my first date with the second man I would marry, three years later.

Another example of change is when you depend on

something and it doesn't always work out. That was how I felt about my church affiliation. I thought my peers would watch over me, but I wasn't wanted. I looked for a new church and found younger couples happy to have me join their group. I had to go through a membership class to join this church—but at that same time the Jonestown Massacre occurred and so religion was a huge factor. I had to be very sure of my commitment of faith! A book about the Jonestown Massacre, nonfiction, *Seductive Poison* by Deborah Layton, will help you understand my concern.

It wasn't easy being single after twenty-seven years of marriage, when your children are pretty much independent. This part of my widowhood I would just as soon like to forget, but my book club friends said I should include it in my book. It began right after I was widowed. He was a friend of my late husband and me, with his wife, and also lived in our neighborhood. He would come over to my home between 10:00 and 10:30 P.M. when I would be getting ready for bed. It was hard to convince him that no meant no with regard to his coming in! He wanted to help me; he said I needed a man. He wanted to help with yard work. He tried to get close to me but I was on guard! Becoming frustrated with what I could do about this situation, I got an idea! We both worked in a downtown area and I also knew his birthday date, which was soon. I called him at his office and said I would like to take him for lunch on his birthday. He was delighted! Next, I called his wife and invited her and told her not to say anything, that we would surprise him. We would meet him in the lobby of his building. I wished I'd had a video camera to capture the look on his face when he got out of the elevator and saw me standing with is wife. After that, he never bothered me again!

Dating was sometimes a wonderful experience. I had dates with a TV anchorman, truck driver, business owner, ex-hockey player, then a banker, a judge, and two men who were fifteen and ten years younger than me. Having a younger man is not all that bad because women usually live longer.

I had the opportunity to go on many dates, but at forty-five, my mind was made up on what I liked in a partner. This person could not be a smoker, and had to drink moderately. He should have good manners, enjoy the outdoors, take care of his appearance and his health, and, most of all, have faith in God. Maybe I was asking too much, but I did meet someone with those qualifications.

His name was Dick, and he was an engineer for the computers where I worked. I had seen him come into the store for years, but we'd never spoken before. I thought he was a sales representative, with his attaché case. I didn't realize his case held his tools.

One day, he stopped at my counter and asked if I would meet him for a drink after work. This was a learning experience for me, first about his traumatic divorce and the mess he was in, because he had made a poor choice of a mate, and after our drinks at the restaurant, when I offered to fix dinner at my home and have him meet my boarder. We went together in my car. I wanted to learn more about Dick.

After arriving home, I got a call from my daughter, who was living off campus, across town. She needed some things from the house since she was going to see her boyfriend in Ann Arbor. So, without having any dinner, Dick came with me to deliver her things.

When we arrived, my daughter asked if I would iron a blouse for her while she finished packing. She noticed I was acting a bit silly and I told her about my date. On our way back to my house, I got sick and had to pull the car over to throw up, several times. Dick took over the driving and took me home where I immediately went to bed and fell asleep.

A bit later I woke up and wondered why the lights in the house were on. I discovered Dick was still there, watching T.V. It was 1:30 A.M. and my boarder had gone to bed without feeding Dick anything. Dick said he was worried about me and wanted to make sure I was all right. We were both very hungry, so I made breakfast and drove him back to his car.

What I found out that evening over drinks was like tuning into a soap opera. Dick had been unhappy for some time with his marriage of twenty-eight years, and had recently met a woman through his work who was very attractive and exciting! After a nasty divorce and losing the trust of his grown children, he was hurting financially. His daughters were married, his son was a junior at Michigan State; Dick paid for his education, but his son needed extra funds, and his dad couldn't help. I wished Dick well and hoped he could work things out.

A few weeks later, my boarder called me at work from Grand Valley to say she couldn't get her motorcycle startled and did I know anyone with a truck. Dick was the only one I knew with a truck, but I suggested my boarder make the call for help herself. Then she asked if she couldn't pay him for his help, would it be okay to fix him dinner? So I fixed dinner for all of us. When they arrived with the motorcycle, I had dinner ready.

Just as we sat down to start, Dick offered to say the blessing. What can I say? I was happy with Dick and hoped his life would turn around. Was this him starting to walk with his Lord?

Later I heard from Dick that he had taken a temporary assignment with his company in North Carolina. He thought it would help his wife in a new environment as she was also in therapy. However, she was not happy and served him with divorce papers soon after they moved to North Carolina. Dick came back to Michigan after his assignment and since he flew his plane home to Michigan, he needed a ride to his house to get his car. I helped him. I had been busy with my daughter's wedding the month before, but just then things were very quiet in my life. Still, the garbage was back, as his soon-to-be-ex was causing trouble, damaging my car and his plane. I had a hard time believing someone could be so wicked. I asked for some proof. Dick called his son to come to my home, not knowing why. The things were true and as I found out later from experience, his ex cheated, lied, stole his property, and Dick almost lost his job of twenty-five years because of her. This attractive woman was very clever, irrational, exciting, and very impractical! I suggested he remarry the mother of his children to heal wounds. But this was not to be.

Dick wanted to turn his life around! I haven't said anything about it, but I think Dick was a good person who had made some bad decisions. I liked him. We started to make plans to get married in June, six months later, after his divorce. We met with my minister and were picking out a date when the minister told us he couldn't marry us unless we moved the date up a few months. Dick had never been one to go to church. Yet he liked the minister of my church, so we picked out an earlier date for our wedding since my minister was leaving for the Crystal Cathedral in California on April 1. We planned for the wedding to take place in a month.

Dick was influenced by my strong faith. Our wedding day was a beautiful warm day. The sad part was Dick's father came to the wedding but not the reception. His mother wanted to come, but his father would not allow it—she had been in the hospital, but was home doing fine. Dick's oldest daughter was upset with her father and skeptical of his decision. She and her husband did not come.

After the wedding, we had close family and friends for lunch at the Amway Grand Plaza, in Grand Rapids, Michigan. We did not know bringing our two grown families together would be so difficult. His mother did say, to me, that her son had become very happy after years of frustration and unhappiness. Our wedding took place on March 5, 1983. On our way to Florida, where we spent our honeymoon, we stopped to see my new mother-in-law. I gave her my wedding bouquet.

I became an instant grandmother, to my delight, which I worked at with no success. I soon felt like the wicked witch of the north. The gatherings at my new husband's grandchildren's birthdays were so upsetting to the ex-wife, I felt, because of me. We suggested to his children that their mother needed them more, because she was alone, so we would stay away.

After our honeymoon, I went back to work. My job of fifteen years had been good for me. I could buy clothes for my family and household items at a discount. The pay wasn't great, but as a department head I learned to take on many responsibilities. Pricing, inventory, knowing the stock, keeping the displays neat, and waiting on customers kept me busy. I did note some jealousy at work, and was getting hours I hadn't had to work before. I had also been cheated on my time card, hours I had worked but not been paid for. I consulted an attorney about this, and he told me this company was notorious for this, if I wished to sue. The attorney also mentioned it could involve and hurt some of my dear friends at work, which made me decide just to quit. It was the first of June.

I had a good summer nevertheless, working hard to get acquainted with my new family and buying and moving into a home that needed lots of fixing up. I found my husband had many talents and did them well. He painted inside and outside. We insulated, had new carpet installed in the master bedroom, had the kitchen remodeled, and Dick added a carport. He owned a small airplane which we flew to upper Michigan. Dick later sold his plane and started building a kit plane, which he never finished because of our move up north. Because of our many projects, I was very busy.

When fall came, I needed something else to do, so I put in my application to some stores at a mall nearby. Two weeks went by and I never got a call. So I went back to the want ads. I love children and noticed many ads for child care. I answered an ad but before going for my interview, I called my church for a recommendation. Neither minister was in so I was rather nervous, because at that time there had been so much in the news about child molestation in child care facilities.

My interview went very well. I had the qualifications and honesty the mother wanted. This was one of the most rewarding times in my life as well as for my new husband. This family became our family. The children were aged three-and-one-half years and eight months. I worked with educational toys, read books to the children, played store, even had their dog, Hershey, deliver mail. I went walking, biking, sledding, and out to lunch with the children. My husband and I were accepted and loved by this family. These children are now young adults and the oldest has a career. This helped so much at a time we were not very welcome by my husband's children. I still find it difficult to make any kind of plans with his children.

When my youngest daughter and her family moved to Grand Rapids, she wanted me to care for my two grandsons while she finished law school. What a joy! But at the same time my parents had health problems and were losing their mobility, so we had to find time to give a lot of care to my parents.

We had purchased some property on a lake in northern Michigan and were thinking of building a moderate summer place. But the cost was too much, so we decided to sell our home and build a home up north. It was a great move, mostly because of the stress from my parents. I was having some health problems as well. My daughter's law school and taking the bar exam and passing was completed before our move. Also, this daughter and her husband were building a home in a different city and would be moving so we moved up north to our new retirement home.

My husband painted the house and built a beautiful deck, where we watched many kinds of birds. We found a new church family and Dick found his Savior Jesus Christ and the faith he needed in his life. He joined this new church. To test Dick's faith, our new church was going into a building project and needed the congregation to think about what they could pledge for the project. It was a big undertaking and people from the church volunteered their homes for small group meetings to talk over ways to pay for this project. Before we arrived at this meeting, we wanted to help, but were concerned about our situation. We were retired and my husband was paying alimony. Our finances were tight. When my husband explained our situation, a woman asked how this could change. Dick said, if his ex would die or remarry. Then the same woman asked if he ever prayed that his ex-wife would remarry and he answered that he never prayed for himself.

This group of people from our new church prayed for Dick that his wife would re-marry. Two weeks later, he got a call from his ex that she was getting married. Our prayers were answered! The church got a nice pledge from us.

Our years up north were wonderful for almost ten years. We did the landscaping, and my husband was close to ideal hunting grounds. I had joined a garden club and was interested in wild flowers and ferns. I had planted almost all species from that area in our yard. Also, I volunteered as chaplain at the local hospital, did highway pick-up, and volunteered at a second-hand shop, the money from sales benefitting to those less fortunate in our area.

Our new church fulfilled our spiritual needs and we made many new friends, some with whom we still communicate. My husband has this church to thank for getting back into music. The music department of our church wanted to form a band and asked people who had played an instrument to help out with a band. It had been forty-one years since my husband had played the clarinet. He soon was playing for three community bands in the area. A first-chair clarinet player in one of the bands heard his playing and asked him to try out for a concert wind group out of Traverse City, Michigan. He made the grade and soon invested in a fine new clarinet.

We were enjoying all the pleasures of music when my husband and a few musicians were getting a swing band together, which was going strong at the time of our next move. We kept up with family and our elderly parents by visiting once a month.

In September 1996 my husband's father died leaving his mother feeling lost and wanting to die herself. She died the next year, in June of 1997, and then my mother passed away in July of 1997. Before that time, people built a house in the lot next to us who were trying to bring the suburbs to a quiet rural setting. Their radio playing was always loud and every piece of yard equipment available would run sometimes for hours. I was very upset and felt I could not live where the people next door were *not* neighborly or considerate of their neighbors. I also missed the grandchildren. I wanted to move, but to where? I thought, back to Grand Rapids closer to our children and grandchildren. After being by water, my husband wanted to stay by water. So we moved to a condo almost surrounded by water. We did have to scale down, but I think at our age, it was a good choice. What did our families think? My children were delighted, and we enjoyed so much more contact with them and are able to help each other. We have found a wonderful church and friends. I have been a volunteer tutor in the grandchildren's school and also teach the fourth graders how to knit. I also volunteer for Hospice of Muskegon Oceana County.

Dick found a rehearsal the first week we were here in a concert band, eighty-something-strong, which he really enjoys. He is also in a woodwind quintet, something he had wanted to do for a long time. He did have an interest in airplanes and owned three at different times. He also joined a plane club, sharing expenses with others. He started to build two planes, not finishing either one because of our moves. Eventually, the medication he was taking determined he was not allowed to fly. However, the cost was getting out of hand, so it was time to go on to other things, and that was music! Dick also plays in several swing bands around the area, which I just remembered I did not put down in my own information questionnaire.

The people who influenced my life were grade school teachers, my father's parents, and an elderly neighbor. God is very important in my life, for he has helped me make wise decisions. When my sister died, I felt so frustrated that I couldn't help her make better choices. When Brother Bob was gone, I knew I needed to spend more time with the family I have. Mementos from my parents, picked after they were both deceased, are cherished—some pieces of furniture, figurines, and my mother's sewing projects.

Next, I thought I would tell you about my children's weddings. Our son was the first to announce he had given his girl an engagement ring. He had not known this girl very long, and though I was very excited, my late husband was worried. He said they did not know each other well enough. I helped with the planning, because the bride's parents were away on a sabbatical.

When the invitations went out, I thought all was going well. After the wedding, I found out the bride's father had given my late husband that letter from my sister, Laura, that was very nasty, calling us unfit parents and saying their daughter would be marrying below her class. That hurt, but when I showed the letter to my parents, I was just brushed off.

The wedding itself was a fainting episode: first the groom fainted twice, so the minister told someone to get a couple of chairs for the bride and groom. The ceremony continued, until the best man fainted. The wedding was in March, which is generally cool, but the temperature was in the high seventies and the church was very warm. My husband was right—the marriage lasted only four years.

The next wedding, of my son, had only two witnesses and the minister, who was my brother, present. I was not asked to attend. That marriage lasted much longer, but never brought any grandchildren into my life. I had been looking forward to being a grandmother. While they were still married, my youngest daughter got married. A big church wedding was planned. The groom was from out of state.

The day of the wedding, my middle daughter, the bride, and me, the mother of the bride, were getting ready and gathering things we had to take to the church. We overlooked some of the candles, and when I checked with the lady who decorated the church, she said we did not have enough candles. I looked for my younger brother to drive me home, since I had very little time before the ceremony would start. I felt we had left some of the candles on the shelf at home. When I couldn't find him, I drove myself, all dressed up, to get the candles.

As I said, time was short, so any red light I came to I would stop and then proceed if no cars were coming. I made it in record time, bringing candles we overlooked to church. It was a gratifying time for me, but also lonely, for I had to drive myself to the reception.

This daughter and her husband had my first three grandchildren. A few years had passed since my son's second divorce and his second wife had fallen in love with a friend of theirs who had lost his wife in a car accident. When he called us to come meet a new girlfriend, just by his voice we knew he'd met someone of whom he was very proud and loved very much. She had two teenagers, and because of my negative experience with stepchildren, I gave him lots of advice!

One day, a couple of months later, I got a call from my son, who asked if I remembered that advice about stepchildren. He reassured me things were good. The son of his new friend had called to ask him to his All-Sports Banquet instead of his biological father. I had to agree that was very unusual.

The day of their wedding we arrived at the wedding site and asked who was picking up my mother. There was a mix-up and so my husband and I went to get my mother. The staff at the nursing home had been notified to have Mother ready, but had forgotten. Mother asked why I was dressed up, and I told her it was my son's wedding day. Mother realized she was not dressed properly and a staff member helped me get her ready within ten minutes. Then we quickly got her into the wheelchair and out the door. My son and his bride were married, and even though it was a little tough at times, they have gotten through by working out their problems with love.

The day came that his grandmother got to hold his son before she died four months later. Of course, I was so happy for my son, too, because being a father has been a wonderful part of his life.

That gives the sense of where I am with my life, with all its blessings. Now I'll tell you about my brother, Bob, the fifth sibling.

IX
Fifth Born

Bob was born March 16, 1936 in a rented house just west of the city of Grand Rapids. I was four years old and don't remember much until our brother, Dean, was born two years later. Bob was a rather quiet child and stayed that sort of personality as he matured. He loved nature! His school days were taken in stride and all went well through high school.

Bob enjoyed fishing, especially fly-fishing. He was the first in my family to hunt. I remember the first deer Bob shot and how delicious it was, and how he did the skinning and cutting himself. But first he was off to college, taking a course in forestry at Michigan State. He met Virginia at our church and gave her a ring on the Fourth of July, 1959. They were married in November of that year in a beautiful church wedding and reception. He and his wife lived in married housing until 1961 when my brother, Dean, and I helped them move to a small house in Traverse City, Michigan.

Bob got his first job in forestry. The job was too seasonal for a good income, so they moved back to Grand Rapids. There, he got a job at the water filtration plant doing water testing in many areas of the city, run off from creeks and such. Their first child, Julie, was born in February of 1965. Then, in August 1966, another girl, Amy, was born. It was a busy time for these young parents and much time was spent outdoors with their girls. Bob's life was cut short, however, for he died of cancer on February 7, 1972 after only twelve years of marriage, leaving a loving wife, Ginny, along with Julie, age seven, and Amy, age five. His wife's fondest memory was Bob walking through the woods, a big smile on his face, with Julie on his shoulders.

Bob was a helpful and loving father. The year that our mother and dad celebrated their fiftieth anniversary, my siblings and I got together to plan a party.

Bob would lead the way planning, with help from his siblings. This brought him very close to his parents, and his death the following year took a very serious toll on my parents. Bob's final days were spent in the hospital, and at that time, for a reason I could never explain until just recently, my brother-in-law, the chiropractor, and my sister, Laura, came to see my brother. My brother-in-law was trying to help my brother with his severe back pain. He gave Bob several treatments, which helped for a very short time. One interesting fact that Bob's wife informed me about when I told her I was writing a book about my family was that when she was first married and living in married housing on campus, she invited my sister, Laura, and her husband over for a visit. Laura and her husband suggested that they should not have children! I am ashamed of not being closer to Bob's wife during her time of grief. My parents were very helpful and her parents were available to help, too.

Bob had been very aware of our environment and the need to take care of our streams, lakes, and forests. I am sorry I did not share more time with him.

Many years passed before Sister Laura had any further contact with our sister-in-law, our brother's widow.

Then on September 10, 1994, Laura decided to come to this deceased brother's daughter's wedding and reception—a first for her of any niece's or nephew's wedding. I explained how I handled that encounter in the chapter about me. I found out later that Laura had called our brother, Harold, and asked what she should do about the invitation to her niece's wedding and reception. I wish I had an answer to a question like that.

After I had written my book, my brother's widow passed away. I had previously told her I had written a book about my family and she wanted to read the chapter on her husband. I had asked her for information and she wrote a very touching letter to me, which helped. She died January 30, 2003, two days after reading that chapter. I understand she told her daughter that I had forgotten one of their moves, but otherwise liked what I had written.

X
Sixth Born

On February 23, 1938, my brother, Dean, was born; my folks were still renting. He would be the sixth and last child, an even three girls and three boys.

Dean was a darling baby and had beautiful blond, curly hair and bright blue eyes! Dean and Bob were two years apart, but as they grew up many people thought they were twins. It's funny how a memory of something that happened many years ago will come to surface. One experience Dean had when he was around ten years old brought laughter and meat to the supper table. Dean was sitting on a fence just passing the time away, throwing stones at nothing in particular, when a rabbit hopped into his sight. Dean took aim at the rabbit, hit it, and killed it. Feeling bad, he headed for home. Our mother noticed right away something was bothering him and asked him what was the matter. He was reluctant to say anything, but did finally come clean. Mother sent him to find the rabbit, and she would fix it for dinner.

In Dean's school days he was a Yo-Yo champion. When dismantling things from my parent's home, we found the vest he had won for being the best in our school. After high school he joined the navy, as he was a very carefree person. After his service, most of his friends were already married. He asked if we knew any girls, and my late husband and I introduced him to a babysitter who was then off to college but came home on weekends. Her parents were our neighbors. They dated a few years and got married on April 3, 1964. They had an elaborate church wedding with a dinner reception. My daughter, Kathy, was the flower girl.

We saw Dean and his family quite often; we even went camping together. Later, Dean bought a cottage, and each year since 1978, the year my late husband died, the family celebrated the Fourth of July there. The last get-together at Dean's cottage was on July 4, 1988. Our father hardly knew what was going on and was in much pain. I had suggested to my siblings that we celebrate a picnic at our parent's home so my dad didn't have to travel, having had the experience of taking him often to appointments and a few outings. My father found it hard to travel because of the pain while riding in the car. My siblings disagreed, so I declined to be a part of that celebration at my brother's cottage with my parents. It was the last time with both parents alive that we spent a Fourth of July together as a family.

After my late husband died, I saw less and less of Dean and his family. When I remarried, it became very plain to me that Dean was not interested in me or my family. When he turned fifty, I surprised him by having his brother and sister-in-law and my husband meet at a restaurant for dinner, in his hometown, Lansing. I was still trying to keep communications open.

Dean's wife inherited her parent's summer home on Lake Michigan and has had a couple of Fourth of July potlucks again for all the siblings and their families. My family has a difficult time with communication. Sharing in family needs is unheard of. Dean seems to shut us out of his life. This youngest brother did not want to answer my questionnaire. It took a couple of phone calls and a letter before he came through. Who influenced him the most? He answered, his brother, Bob, then later his older brother, Harold, and his peers at work and with those he plays (golf). Getting a new bike and sled were the best things to happen to him as a child. My youngest brother said his wife was also a great influence in his life. He was an engineer, which was his greatest achievement, passing the state exam. God is a very private matter with this youngest brother.

The death of his sister did not effect Dean because, at that time in his life, he was rather carefree. He wrote that when our brother, Bob, passed away, it was terrible because his brother was such a fine person in every way. He couldn't remember any particular story, so the rabbit story will be a surprise to him! He was surprised to receive the money our folks left to him, for he thought they were poor.

An expression you hear once in a while is, you can pick your friends, but you're stuck with family. I have tried, but have had little success, keeping communications flowing. You may think my life rather sad, but it taught me many lessons. I had so many things to be thankful for, and the way to go is with the teachings of Jesus, more then riding on God's coattails!

I have presented all of my family members and feel life for us would be much better if we would all be honest, helpful, and open when sharing each others' concerns. I remember a song we sang in Sunday school, "We should trust and obey, for there's no other way, or what would Jesus do?"

XI
Leaving a Heritage and Staying on God's Coattails!

I want to finish my book talking about how individuals can plan ahead as to how they would like their cherished heirlooms distributed. It takes greed out of the picture, which may arise in any family.

My parents were very frugal! They did not share with us the many wonderful things they had acquired, where they came from, or who had made some of the items. My mother wanted my youngest daughter to have her good set of dishes and crystal. She also gave her the master bedroom set, but before that my youngest daughter had asked if she could buy the dining room set which included a table, eight chairs, china cabinet, and buffet. A few other outdoor chairs and an old secretary they (my parents) had antiqued were also given to this granddaughter.

My oldest brother was storing in his basement what was left of my parents' household goods. He didn't seem to be concerned about taking care of those items. My two brothers with our mates finally got together and started to sort things out. My mother was still living at the time, so when I discovered some very old doilies, a crocheted necktie, an apron (fancy), and bed hat, I washed, starched, and mended them and brought them to have her tell me to whom they belonged. The beautiful floor-length apron was made by my grandmother (my mother's mom) when she was in her teens. It was over one hundred years old, as was a crocheted necktie belonging to my mother's father. I have framed some of those doilies as keepsakes for my daughter and daughter-in-law.

I had not seen any of these items of my mother's before. When it came time to choose what we would each like to have, I wanted a drop-leaf table that was badly warped and water-marked from plants, a small lamp table with the same water-marked top, and a cedar chest (yes, also with a water-marked top). The three pieces were refinished for a reasonable price. I also took my mother's treadle sewing machine, thinking my husband could fix it up, but parts went to an attic dealer. My brother kept the figurines until we had a place for them, but when I went to get them, my youngest brother's wife had taken them. I was afraid I was too late, but did get them back, for which I was very thankful. My brothers wanted me to take a few pieces of jewelry, vases, and all of my mother's sewing projects. I found pieces my mother had cut and some put together for a quilt she started back in the 1940s. I am proud to say, never having quilted before, that I made a full-size quilt for our guest bedroom, with pillowslips to match.

There was a china doll head found in our parents' belongings and none of us knew to whom it belonged. Later, when I brought the various handmade items—apron, mom's father's crocheted necktie and such—to have my mother tell me who made them, I asked about the china doll head. Mother said it was hers. I was telling my daughter about it and she said she would love to have it because she had a friend who made bodies and clothes for antique dolls. She wanted it for a keepsake. When I inquired about the doll, my sister-in-law would not answer, and to this day I do not know what happened to it.

Next came letters, cards, photos, framed pictures, clothing, and some linen. I took out the photos and, after sorting through, gave those of my siblings present what they wanted. I made up eleven packages for those who might be interested in having them. I received one reply, with a "thank you."

I have encouraged my children to ask for things from our household that they would like and appreciate when we are gone, to keep them in our family. I have made a complete inventory, so if there is any history with an item, it is written down.

I have many photo albums documenting our life with family and friends. I hope someday one of my children will take an interest. My second husband's mother gave me a set of china and silver plate flatware, and it is in our will that they go to his daughters.

The past is important and how we carry on traditions, relationships, and showing we care about our heritage. I found so many questions unanswered that I wanted my children and grandchildren to know that sharing in all things is very satisfying and important!

One thing I want to mention is how I have heard over and over again stories of older adults offering to their families or friends different objects from their households. It would make them very happy if those who are offered a gift would take it and be grateful. Just think, they like you enough to give you something.

All this has been written so those who read this book might take stock of their lives and help those in their family ask questions before it is too late. Be willing to share—families do much better in their lives with great communication! Everyone who is of sound mind and body should take responsibility for their lives, and don't wait too long! We can then help those who are less fortunate. Teaching good manners and responsibility, and emphasizing the love of God to our children is so important. Let there be love in your home. Help our country back to "In God We Trust." This is why I ride on God's coattails!

Questionnaire

I sent a questionnaire to my three surviving siblings to help fill in some memories and information I would not know otherwise because I was born fourth. These are the questions:

1. Where were you born?
2. Who influenced you the most on how you live?
   a. Father
   b. Mother
   c. A Teacher
   d. Other
3. Is God important in your life?
4. The best thing that happened to you as a child?
5. The best thing that happened to you as an adult?
6. What impact on your life did losing your sister, Dorothy, have?
7. What impact on your life did losing your brother, Bob, have?
8. What is your favorite memory or tale about your family?
9. What keepsake is important to you left by your parents?

I hope by asking these questions it will also help you understand the different personalities.